Italy

GEORGE KISH

AROUND THE WORLD PROGRAM

Prepared with the cooperation of the
American Geographical Society

ITALY is a land of yesterdays and of tomorrow. Past and present are so intermingled that the visitor finds it a little hard to decide whether it is a Roman ruin, a medieval church, or a brand-new shop that will claim his attention. And over this strange and fascinating mixture of old and new there is a spirit that is strictly of our time. In spite of its antiquities, Italy is very much alive.

Italy is an "island". Surrounded on three sides by water, separated on the fourth side from the rest of Europe by the highest mountains of the continent, it appears as isolated at first glance as any country could be. But these seas and mountains have never been real barriers. Men sailed across the seas and marched through the mountain passes to countries in northern Europe, in western Asia, in northern Africa. It is a paradox that Italy, a seemingly isolated country, has always been in intimate contact with others, and has made such a significant contribution to Europe and to the world in art, literature, science, and government.

The Italian Boot

GENERATIONS of schoolboys learned that Italy is shaped like a boot, and no one has as yet succeeded in bettering that stock phrase. Alpine mountain wall in the north; rich, fertile, wedge-shaped Po Valley lying between the Alpine arc and the arc of the wild and craggy Appennine Mountains, sweeping south-east through the whole penin-

3

sula. From Italy's most northern point in the heart of the Alps to the southern tip of the boot it is about 760 miles. From the blue Adriatic on the east to the even bluer Tyrrhenian Sea on the west, across the peninsula, it is about 150 miles on the average. To the south the toe of the boot seems to be kicking one of two large islands, Sicily. The other, Sardinia, west of the peninsula, completes the roster of Italy.

Geography was, beyond doubt, of importance in shaping the people of Italy. In a land that never has had many trees, stones became the prime medium of man. The granites of the Alps, the priceless marbles of Tuscany, the easily shaped volcanic rocks near Rome lent themselves readily to architect, mason, sculptor. Whether it was the primitive stone towers that stand on the lonely, windswept heights of Sardinia; the impressive sweeping arches of the Colosseum; the finely carved facades of Venetian palaces; or the statues and busts of Roman Emperors, medieval soldiers of fortune, and Renaissance figures of elegance: all these were products of Italian stone, Italian imagination.

In the framework provided by nature, on a stage that provides such variety for the actors, the drama of Italian history has taken place. This drama spans the entire period of Western civilization.

Greek Coins and Etruscan Arches

THE WRITTEN HISTORY of Italy begins nearly 3,000 years ago when merchants, farmers, and fishermen of Greece settled on the coasts of southern Italy and Sicily. Soon, their cities achieved such prosperity that they were called "Greater Greece", having surpassed their homeland in trade, in learning, and in the arts. Some of the Greek settlements still stand: Naples, Italy's third-largest city, now a swarming metropolis with nearly 1.2 million people, is one of them — the "Neapolis", or "New Town" of Greek fame. Many others have disappeared as their walls and buildings crumbled into dust. But here and there in Italy the visitor comes across a Greek temple whose slender columns blend into the landscape, part of it, rather than defacing it. The Italian farmer, hoeing his garden, occasionally strikes a coin which, when cleaned and polished, still shows a classical Greek profile.

Earthenware, brightly painted, is popular with Italians and tourists. Here a craftsman is decorating a plate, working in his shop that is workroom, display and salesroom at the same time.

13.   PAINTING POTTERY IN AMALFI

North of the Greek settlements another people, the Etruscans, built their towns and cities on the hilltops of central Italy. Their language is unknown to us, and neither do we know whence they came. But their finely wrought bronze statues and their pottery show that the Etruscans were expert craftsmen, whose skills have been transmitted to Italians who live today on the sites of ancient Etruscan settlements. The rounded arch first appeared in Etruscan buildings, and has been part of architecture on Italian soil ever since that time.

Rome Was Not Built in a Day

THE LATINS, who lived in the Tiber River Valley, and were looked down upon by the Etruscans on their borders, as simple herdsmen and farmers, founded Rome, their first town, in the year 753 B.C. That is the tradition, at any rate. But Rome was not built in a day, as the old

saying goes. For the first centuries of its existence, Rome was a small rather unimportant market town, at an easy ford on the Tiber. Through a series of successful wars Rome extended its rule over the nearby countryside, over all of Italy, later still over the entire Mediterranean until, at the time of the birth of Christ, the Roman Empire included what is now England, France, Spain, Switzerland, south Germany, Austria, Hungary, the Balkans, as well as Turkey, Syria, and North Africa.

The Romans were a strong, upright people. Whatever they may have lacked in the way of artistic gifts, they certainly made up in military prowess, in a knack for good administration, and in their genius for law. Roman law is probably the most lasting monument the Romans built, and the most widely influential. And while the law of England and of the United States followed a course very different from that of the rest of Europe, where Roman law is still all-important, no lawyer could dispense with a few terms and phrases that were current in Roman courts 2,000 years ago. "Habeas corpus", a cornerstone of our civil liberties, is itself a Latin phrase.

A Network of Roads

I T WOULD BE IMPOSSIBLE to imagine Italy without the visible and invisible imprint of Rome. The Romans were ingenious and prolific

The Roman Empire was held together by a splendid road system, and Roman roads were the first Europe had ever known. In Italy there are remnants of the original pavement still to be found; this is the Via Flaminia, the road from Rome to the Adriatic Sea.

7

The Appian Way, "the queen of the roads", stretches to the distant hills; a flock of sheep wends its way homeward, and the winter sun is gilding the trunks of tall poplars along the roadside.

builders. The Roman passion for baths left public bathing establishments that are still impressive by their size. The Roman Emperors' custom of offering free entertainment resulted in such monuments as the Colosseum of Rome; the well-paved and well-maintained highways of the Empire made road building an Italian tradition. Over the centuries a spider web of solid, well built Roman roads linked all parts of the far-flung Empire. Italians are still building superior highways. A tremendous new one called the Road of the Sun, l'Autostrade del Sole, a superb 460 mile four-lane express road linking Milan with Naples through Rome, is one completed in recent years.

For 400 years, from the time of Julius Caesar to the fifth century of the Christian era, the Roman Empire ruled Italy and the vast lands in Europe, Asia, and Africa. During that time Christianity became the official religion of the Empire, and the bishop of Rome became the head of the Church. To this day, the Pope retains that title, and his residence is still in Rome. The power of the Empire waned, however, and by 400 A.D. many of the territories were conquered by people whom the Romans called "barbarians".

In the year 476, the last Roman Emperor lost his throne, most of his power having been taken over earlier by the Emperor of the East, who resided in Constantinople (also called Byzantium). By that time Italy itself was invaded, Rome and many other cities were looted, and the unity of Italy was destroyed. For 1,400 years after that, Italy was a divided land.

During the centuries that followed the country was ruled by foreigners. The Lombards, and later, the Franks, people of German origin, held the north and much of central Italy. The Byzantine Emperors of Constantinople were the lords of the east coast. Arabs ruled over Sicily and its rich farmlands. Rome, once a city of a million people, became a vast empty shell, with about 30,000 inhabitants. The palaces and arenas stood empty, the public meeting places were used as fortresses, the abandoned farmlands changed into malarial swamp or rough pasture.

The Age of City-states

Two SEAPORTS, Venice, at the head of the Adriatic in the north, and Amalfi, near Naples, on the Tyrrhenian Sea in the south, were the only places not under foreign rule. But Amalfi fell to the Normans early in the twelfth century, and later a large part of the city was de-

The tiny hill town of San Gimignano, in Tuscany, looks like a miniature skyscraper city from the distance. Its thirteen towers, each, in the past, the fortified retreat of a family, are all that remains of the former glory of this once independent city-state.

9. SAN GIMIGNANO, HILL TOWN IN TUSCANY

stroyed. Venice, protected by the waters of the sea, prospered and became the greatest sea power and the wealthiest city of Italy.

The example of Venice, a city of islands, was followed by the cities of the mainland: Florence, Milan, Siena, and many other towns became independent republics, governed by councils of their own citizens. Some of the city-states were quite sizable, ruling over extensive territory beyond their walls: Florence and Milan were among the most prominent of these. Others were tiny, picturesque republics whose rule was limited to the hilltop where the town itself was built, like the medieval village of San Gimignano in Tuscany, near Florence, where now about 3,500 people live among the ancient walls, palaces and towers, that were medieval fortress homes.

The conflicts between these cities, and the strife that divided the people within their walls, became an important feature of Italian life. The bitter rivalry between Capulet and Montague that Shakespeare portrayed in "Romeo and Juliet", could have been found in any Italian city of the Middle Ages. The thirteen towers of San Gimignano are the last remnants of many more such fortified houses, where the citizens retired to defend themselves whenever civil war threatened.

8.   MARKET PLACE, VERONA

Every morning the main square of Verona, the town of Romeo and Juliet, is filled with the stands of merchants and farmers, holding open-air market under their great white umbrellas.

Spices, Silk and Bankers

THE POWER AND WEALTH of the Italian cities was founded on trade. Venice and Genoa, the two great sea powers of medieval Europe, shared between them most of the commerce between East and West. Spices, silks, precious stones were carried by Venetian and Genoese ships from Egypt and the Arab Near East to their home ports, to be shipped on across the Alps to Germany, or by sea to France, Flanders, and England. As profits accumulated, the financial power of the Italian cities increased, until they were the source of money for much of Europe. In our word "bank" there is an echo of this age: the word comes from "banco", the Italian term for bench, where the money-changers and moneylenders sat in the town square.

To the rest of Europe, this time of Italian prosperity meant a great deal in other ways, too. The wealth amassed in the Italian cities became the foundation of a Golden Age of arts and letters that was the greatest Europe had ever seen. "Renaissance", the term most often used to describe it, means rebirth, or a return to the artistic and literary traditions of the Greek and Roman world. But it really meant much more. In a practical sense, it might be said that the Renaissance created works of great and lasting beauty that are still the glory of Italy and of our Western civilization.

"Renaissance": the Arts in Italy

THE RENAISSANCE began with the recognition of Italian as a language fit to express thoughts in poetry and in prose. Until the thirteenth century, Latin was the language of poets and historians. But only scholars and churchmen could understand it. But then, about the year 1300, Dante, Italy's greatest poet, wrote in Italian his great poem of life and after-life, the "Divine Comedy", and so established Italian as equal to Latin for all time to come. Dante's contemporary, the painter, Giotto, made a similar "declaration of independence", in painting. The figures on his canvases and wall paintings are living people, moving in an Italian landscape, chatting in front of the buildings of an Italian town, clothed in the Italian fashions of his time. They were not stiff and stylized, in the manner painters had followed for nearly a thousand years.

The Renaissance was the time when architecture, painting, sculpture, and music suddenly shook off the conventions that had governed the arts. Towns and cities became filled with great churches, splendid palaces, squares superbly planned and balanced. Artists competed with each other, supported by the open purses of the enthusiastic towns-people, or of the local prince.

It was an exciting time. And it is truly remarkable that all this flowering of the arts could take place against a background of almost continuous strife that would frequently burst into open warfare. Italy was a divided country, weak and without real power. When Columbus voyaged to America, when England, France, and Spain were mighty monarchies,

united and powerful, Italy consisted of fifteen separate republics, kingdoms, and principalities.

After Columbus, Italy Was Left Behind

WITH THE OPENING UP of the New World, and with the establishment of a sea route to India and the lands of the Orient around Africa, the Mediterranean ceased to be the most important seaway of the Western world. Trade with America was swelling considerably the coffers of both the Spanish and Portuguese merchants and unfortunately not those of Venice and Genoa. At about the same time the Turks, having already taken Constantinople, completed the conquest of Egypt, long the clearinghouse of Italian trade with Asia, and closed much of the Mediterranean to Italian shipping. The successful conquest of all of southern Italy by Spain was the third major blow. By 1550, most of Italy was once more under foreign rule.

This foreign rule lasted for three centuries. Yet arts, letters, and the sciences continued to flourish. The new art of printing, invented in Germany in the fifteenth century, flourished here, and Italian printing presses published books that are still the best examples of the printers' art. The Renaissance, and the Baroque period that followed it, continued to produce great works of art, by great masters.

Italian Artists: Jacks of Many Trades, Masters of All

THE ARTISTS of the sixteenth and seventeenth centures were masters of more than one medium. Leonardo da Vinci, whose "Mona Lisa" and "Last Supper" have been admired for four centuries, was one of the greatest painters. But he was also a mechanical genius who conceived and drew accurate, practical plans for flying machines, tanks, and battleships that are still the wonder of engineers. Michelangelo decorated the ceiling of the Sistine Chapel in Rome with the largest and most famous frescoes of all time. He also designed the magnificent dome of St. Peter's in Rome, and as a sculptor created such immortal masterpieces as his statue of Moses and the tombs of the Medici family. Galileo, physicist,

The "Galleria," Milan.

Statue of David by Bernini, Borghese Gallery, Rome.

Ancient bridge spans the Tiber, Rome.

Ruins of Hadrian's palace, Rome.

Borghese Gardens (245 acres of public park) in Rome.

Arch of Constantine, Rome.

The Via Veneto in Rome.

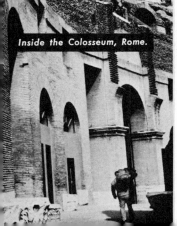
Inside the Colosseum, Rome.

Cafe in Milan's "Galleria."

astronomer, inventor of the telescope, formulated the law of gravity with his famous experiment, allegedly dropping stones from the leaning tower of Pisa. Bernini, architect of some of the most beautiful churches of Rome, was also a sculptor whose admirable fountains are still among the delights of that city.

Allegro, Andante, or Presto: It's All in Italian

AFTER 1500, still another of the arts was added to those practiced by Italians: music. There were earlier composers in Italy, to be sure. But it was during the late Renaissance and Baroque periods that Italian music came to the forefront throughout Europe. Most of our musical vocabulary is Italian, taken over unchanged from the sixteenth century. Whether it is the form of a composition: sonata or concerto; the way it should be played: allegro, andante, adagio; or the volume of the sound that should be employed: pianissimo or forte; or the instruments themselves: violin, viola, cello, piano—we use Italian terms.

Opera is the musical delight of most Italians, and La Scala in Milan is the best and most famous opera house in the country. Toscanini conducted there, and to sing in La Scala is the hallmark of final success to any artist in the world.

19.   LA SCALA OPERA HOUSE, MILAN

From the sixteenth century onward, Italian composers and performers have given the world a continuous stream of great music. Monteverdi, the father of that most Italian of all forms of music, the opera; Palestrina, the first "modern" composer of sacred music; Vivaldi, who created the concerto for orchestra and solo instruments; and the masters of Italian opera: Donizetti, Verdi, Puccini: these names and many others are immortal in music history. In Italy they are kept alive in some of the greatest opera houses of the world, above all in Milan's "La Scala", and in concert halls where good music can be heard all the year round.

Battles for Unity: A New Country Is Born

MODERN, united Italy was born about a century ago, when four men: a king, a philosopher, a soldier, and a statesman put an end to foreign rule over their country. Victor Emmanuel, king of Sardinia and of Piedmont, became the symbol of this new Italy in 1848. Mazzini, poet, philosopher, dreamer, coined the battle cry of "Young Italy" and rallied his countrymen around the new Italian flag. Garibaldi, fighter for freedom, a striking figure in the red shirt he always wore in battle, was the knight of Italian unity who led his men, sometimes against overwhelming odds, in a series of spectacular campaigns that

Anita Garibaldi, wife of the hero of Italian unity, was known and famed as a fighter. Her statue stands on Rome's Gianicolo hill, a short distance from that of her husband.

5. MONUMENT TO ANITA GARIBALDI

overthrew the rulers of south Italy. Cavour, Prime Minister of King Victor Emmanuel, forged the alliances that assured Italy the support of other European nations in the fight for unity. In 1861 Victor Emmanuel became the first king of modern Italy, with northern Turin its capital.

On September 20, 1870, Italian troops stormed the walls of Rome and entered the city. The Pope, last of the rulers on Italian soil to hold out against unity, retired to the Vatican palace, and Rome became Italy's capital. September 20 is Italy's Independence Day. On that day Italy as we know it today was born.

Roman Holiday: Watch the Traffic!

STROLLING on a Roman street, the pedestrian is kept continuously busy watching for cars, buses, trucks, motor scooters (the popular

FLAG OF ITALY

The green, white, and red of the Italian flag were the symbol of Italian unity long before modern Italy was born. Today it is the flag of the young Italian Republic, created in 1946, when the last king of Italy lost his throne by popular vote.

"Vespa" or "Wasp", a name well-earned by their buzzing little engines), carts, bicycles. Gaily painted two-wheeled carts, drawn by sturdy horses, stand in front of taverns, unloading huge casks of wine they have brought from the nearby hills.

Romans and tourists alike find that one of the best ways to enjoy the constantly changing panorama of Roman life is from the terrace of a café. Sipping an espresso, the tiny cup of very strong coffee, one can sit back and watch the rest of Rome hustle by during much of the day. But at one o'clock in the afternoon the streets empty, the flow of traffic dwindles to a trickle: it is the siesta, the noontime break. Stores close their doors, clerks leave their offices, everyone hurries home to enjoy lunch and a rest. It is only after three in the afternoon that life begins anew.

All of this activity takes place in a city that seems to possess only two industries: government and the tourist trade, though in recent years two glamorous new ones have developed to add further interest to the Roman scene. One is making motion pictures, with Rome the most important place for their production in Europe. The other is fashion, in which Rome is second only to Paris in some lines, leads all in others. Rome being the capital of Italy, a large number of its citizens work in one of the many offices that look after the machinery of government. Tourists and pilgrims are attracted to Rome by its works of art, and by the role Rome plays as the seat of the Pope and headquarters of the Catholic Church.

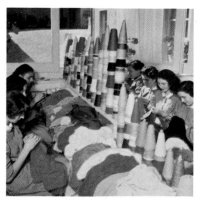

Taste and skill, a keen sense of style, and good modern design are responsible for the recent and spectacular success of Italian fashions. These sweaters, made in Perugia, have become popular all over the world.

15. MAKING ANGORA SWEATERS IN PERUGIA

Stop! You Are Leaving Italy

WITHIN ROME stands the Vatican, a city within a city, the world's smallest sovereign state. It has an area of 108 acres and a permanent population of about a thousand. But on high holidays the great square in front of St. Peter's Church is packed with as many as 300,000 people, straining to catch a glimpse of the Pope, and to receive his blessing. Vatican City was created by treaty in 1929, when the Italian state and the Holy See officially recognized each other's existence. During the previous sixty years, ever since 1870, the Pope was a voluntary prisoner within his palace. Today the Pope is sovereign of the tiny state that includes St. Peter's Church, the great library and famous art mu-

1.   ST. PETER'S CHURCH, ROME

St. Peter's is the largest church in Christendom, and a pilgrimage goal for all Roman Catholics. Its splendid dome, designed by Michelangelo, towers 435 feet, and is 138 feet in diameter; a vast colonnade rises above the square where hundreds of thousands assemble on high holidays, to cheer the Pope and await his blessing.

seum of the Vatican, the residence of the Pope, and the offices of the Roman Catholic Church.

There is only a white line, painted on the pavement of St. Peter's Square, that separates Vatican State from Italy. But the Germans, during their occupation of Rome in 1943-1944, respected Vatican neutrality, and Allied diplomats, representing their countries at the Holy See, were never disturbed as long as they stayed within the Vatican. The Swiss guards stand watch at the gates, in their unique uniforms, designed four centuries ago during the Renaissance, it is believed by the painter Raphael.

Keats and Shelley lived next door to this famous stairway, the Spanish Steps of Rome, built about 1725, that lead to one of the city's many hills. All year round, florists have their stands at the foot of the Spanish Steps.

4. SPANISH STAIRS AND TRINITY CHURCH, ROME

16. CASTLE ST. ANGELO AND BRIDGE ACROSS THE TIBER, ROME

Castle St. Angelo, built in 135 A.D. as the tomb of the Emperor Hadrian, and generally known as Hadrian's tomb, later was a burial place for Roman Emperors, then a fortress of the Popes; today it is a museum, and a landmark of the Roman scene.

Roman Buildings: Pick Your Own Style

ROME is a city that bewilders the tourist, and leaves him at first somewhat overwhelmed. Every style of architecture that has flourished during the last 2,000 years can be found within its walls; incidentally, the walls are real, not merely a figure of speech. The heart of the city is still surrounded on three sides by a set of walls built around 275 A.D., huge walls of solid masonry, pierced by gates and passages. It is an unusual sight to watch modern, motorized traffic sweep through these gates, the same gates through which rumbled the chariots of the Roman Empire, and Allied tanks in 1944.

Much of the front of Rome, its façade, is Baroque: the style that flourished under the Popes between 1550 and 1750. But behind the façade you never know what you may find, for instance, a church interior of the Renaissance, with the high altar in the Gothic style, the whole church surmounting an early medieval crypt which, in turn, was built on a Roman foundation dating back to the time of Christ. One does not have to be an archaeologist or a historian to enjoy it. There is a wonderful vitality about this city, and ruined or intact, all of its buildings are part of its everyday life.

There is also modern Rome, with new apartments, office buildings

Modern architecture is as much part of the Italian scene as the monuments of the past. Rome's great sports ground with its gymnasium, swimming pool, and athletic fields, is one of the city's handsomest examples of contemporary buildings.

14.   ATHLETIC FIELD, ROME

24

12. THE COLOSSEUM, ROME

The Colosseum of Rome, built in 80 A.D., was a giant arena, 160 ft. high, that once held some 50,000 spectators. In spite of the destruction wrought by wars, earthquakes, and men who used its stones for buildings, the Colosseum is still an imposing landmark.

and public buildings, some of them of striking modern design, that contrast dramatically with the ornate and classic façades of ancient and Renaissance Rome. Rome possesses a Europeanized version of Hollywood, too: the Italian film industry, reborn after World War II, made Italian cinema famous the world over, and Italian as well as American films are being made all the time. The cafés of Rome's most fashionable street, the Via Veneto, are haunts of the great and near great of the film industry of two continents, as well as of painters, sculptors, and musicians who flock to the Eternal City as they have done for centuries.

Rome, above all, is the mirror of Italian history. The great public meeting place, the Forum, saw all of the principal figures of the Rome before and during the period of the Roman Empire, and its great ruined temples, archives, triumphal arches have been the happy hunting ground of archaeologists for quite some time now. Tiny churches, hidden in narrow streets far from the busy thoroughfares, their ceilings gleaming with mosaics of a thousand years ago, speak of the time when Rome had fallen on evil days and was reduced to nothing but a small country town.

The richness of the palaces, churches, and the fountains of the Renaissance remind the visitor of the pomp of the Rome of the Popes, who poured their personal fortunes and much of the wealth of the Church into a great and successful effort to make Rome the most beautiful city of their time. The vast marble monument to Victor Emmanuel, first king of Italy, stands, a memorial to the years between 1870 and 1918, years of slow, steady growth under King Victor and his successors. And across from that monument, on a handsome square, stands the palace that was once the Venetian embassy to the Holy See: Palazzo Venezia. There is a tiny balcony that juts out from the front of the palace on the square, and from that balcony Benito Mussolini harangued his followers through the years of Fascism.

Balcony Empire: Italian Fascism

FASCISM was the answer of a good many Italians to the problems and difficulties that beset Italy at the end of the First World War. Italy did not fare too well, in the opinion of her people, in the peace settlements. The turmoil of the postwar years, the rapid rise of strong Socialist and Communist parties, a wave of crippling strikes, disturbed the country profoundly. The Fascist movement offered stability to Italy; public works to absorb the unemployed, a drive for overseas possessions that

appealed to Italians who are fond of the tradition of the Roman Empire. All this was to be theirs, but at a price: rule by one party, led by one man. And while the price did not seem too steep at first, it increased as the years went on, to include the loss of civil liberties, involvement in foreign wars and, finally, the invasion of Italy by the Allies in 1943. That year saw the fall of Mussolini and while his regime survived for a while under German protection in northern Italy, it went down to final defeat in 1945.

Twenty years of Fascism left few marks on Rome, but the country-side around Rome, Lazio, saw some profound changes. Marshes were drained, malaria was brought under control, and empty land was turned into some of the best farms of central Italy.

The political and religious life of Italy depends on Rome: the seat of Parliament, the residence of the President of the Italian Republic, and of the Pope. But the financial and industrial heart of Italy is 400 miles to the north in Milan. Milan with 1.5 million people is the second biggest Italian city, and is the largest city of northern Italy. It was founded by the Romans in a spot where important routes from beyond the Alps came out onto the north Italian plain.

Business and Pleasure Mix Well in Milan

MILAN is a city of industry and finance, of railways and express high-ways. Italy's largest banks have their headquarters there, and the Milan stock market measures the state of Italy's business. There is an activity about the city that is not like the lively bustle of Rome; it reminds one rather of the strenuous work one finds in any home of big business. In and around Milan, in its suburbs and in nearby towns are Italy's most important industrial plants. Steel, automobiles, typewriters, sewing machines, chemicals, textiles, all are represented. And the visitor would do well to remember that Lombardy, the region surrounding Milan, is the largest industrial region of the Mediterranean, of all southern Europe.

Milan is not all industry and high finance and transportation hub, however. The hub of the city is the great square where Milan's cathedral stands, one of Italy's largest churches elaborately ornamented with

CATHEDRAL, MILAN

Milan's cathedral, begun in the fourteenth century but finished in the nineteenth, stands in the heart of the city, a marble mass of pinnacles, arches, and statues, an island of peace in the midst of the swirling traffic of Italy's business capital.

more than one hundred pinnacles and thousands of statues. Begun in the fourteenth century it was not finished for nearly 500 years. Just off Cathedral Square is the famous Gallery, glass-covered, full of shops and cafés where the Milanesi enjoy their after-dinner coffee or early evening drinks, watching the passing parade. Late in the evening "La Scala", badly damaged during World War II, but now superbly restored, offers the best in opera that music lovers could ask for.

The countryside surrounding Milan, the Lombardy Plain, is just as important to Italy's food supply as Milan and other nearby towns are to Italian industry. Long lines of tall poplars, the kind known as Lombardy poplars, stand along the roads that crisscross the fertile plain. The Po River and its tributaries bring abundant water from the Alps, and irrigated fields of wheat and corn, rice and beets stretch clear to the horizon. Further north the Alps and their foothills provide Lombardy with still another source of wealth: the swift Alpine streams are harnessed by many dams to generate electricity for trains, industrial machinery, homes, and farms. But the Alps to the north of Milan give Italy more than hydroelectric power. In mountain valleys set below forest-clad slopes and towering peaks are the lovely Italian lakes of Como, Garda, and Maggiore, resort and vacation regions that draw visitors from everywhere. Soon Milan will be linked to France beyond the Alps by a new road tunnel cut under Europe's highest peak, Mont Blanc. Its construction, a joint Italian-French enterprise, is one of the greatest engineering achievements of modern times.

Piedmont: Champagne and Cars

To the northwest of Lombardy lies Piedmont, the land that led the Italian fight for unity in the battles of 1848, 1859, and 1866. It is even more varied than Lombardy. Highland Piedmont is the wild mountain country of the Alps that attracts tourists from all over Italy, and

Alpine villages like this one lie in the shadow of high peaks; the one which is plainly visible here is Europe's highest, Mont Blanc. Snow slides off easily from the steep roofs, and the stone houses keep warm during the long winter months.

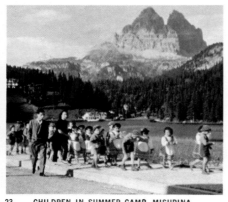

Children from the hot, teeming streets of Italian towns are taken to summer camps high in the Alps. Here, a group of tots are seen against the spectacular background of the "Three Peaks", in the mountains north of Venice.

23.   CHILDREN IN SUMMER CAMP, MISURINA

generates large amounts of hydro-electric power. The low hills of Piedmont around Asti are covered by vineyards that produce a sparkling wine similar to champagne. The Po lowland of eastern Piedmont, near the Lombardy border, is the greatest growing area in Europe.

Turin, the old capital of Piedmont, might best be described as a happy mixture. A brisk and bustling city of more than 900,000 people, it is the home of Fiat, the largest Italian automobile manufacturer; it is also a city of stately boulevards, well-proportioned squares, handsome palaces, with something of a French air about it, for Turin is only a few miles east of the French border and is linked to France by a main highway.

Car-crazy Italians

AUTOMOBILES are one of Italy's leading industries. More than 600,000 were turned out in 1961, of which over 200,000 were exported to other countries. The Italians are fascinated by wheeled vehicles; cars, motorcycles, motor scooters, bicycles are among their most popular products, and the object of many a dream. The Fiat works are the only mass-producing, assembly-line type of automobile plant, but there are quite a few other, smaller companies whose products are known the world over.

Italian racing cars have long been recognized as among the world's best.

For Italians with more modest pocketbooks, who could not afford the shiny, sleek, and powerful cars made by Alfa Romeo, Lancia, and others, the motor scooter provided an answer. Since World War II, Italian motor scooters have proved immensely popular not only within Italy, but throughout much of Europe. They are sturdy, they can carry two adults, a child, and some luggage. For people who cannot even afford a motor scooter, bicycles are the most popular form of transportation. Bicycle racing, particularly long-distance races like the famous "Giro d'Italia" (Tour of Italy), are second only to soccer as popular spectator sports, and all the great cycling champions take an important place in the press, on the radio and in the hearts of the people.

Bologna: Learning and Good Food

South-east of Milan the wide plains of the Po continue all the way to the shores of the Adriatic Sea. These are the plains of Emilia, a region long known for its good farms, for the beautiful churches, for the fine food that some consider the best in Italy. Bologna, with 440,000 people, largest city of Emilia, has been known since the Middle Ages as the "learned city"—it is the seat of Italy's oldest university, founded in the eleventh century and so perhaps the world's oldest university—and it has also been known as the "fat city", whose cuisine stands as a symbol of perfection to connoisseurs of Italian cooking. Bologna lies on the main lines of travel that lead to Florence, Rome, and Naples, yet is bypassed by the vast majority of tourists. Bologna's two leaning towers, its still incomplete and interesting Gothic cathedral, and the arcades that are the chief distinction of all main streets of the city, make it as interesting a town as you would find in northern Italy.

This last statement, however, has to be qualified and seriously so. Not far from Bologna, a hundred miles or less as the crow flies, stands

2.   THE GRAND CANAL, VENICE

The Grand Canal in Venice, 220 feet wide, is where palaces, built during Venice's Golden Age, stand like jewel boxes on the waters' edge. Sleek gondolas, squat steamboats, and swift motorboats crisscross the Canal all day long.

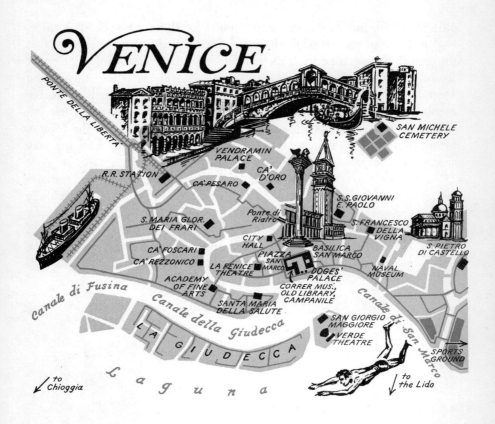

a city unique in Italy and in the world: Venice. The first glimpse of it, as the little steamboat glides away from the landing at the railway station or the end of the highway, is that of a fairy tale. Everything moves by water in Venice: passenger boats that replace cars and buses; the trim black gondolas that are Venice's taxis; the fire department; ambulances, and funerals.

Venice, City Between Water and Sky

V ENICE is built on scores of tiny pieces of land, 117 islets, that stand above the shallow waters of the coastal region. Underpinned by pilings, the churches, palaces, and slums (for there are such in Venice, too) of the city rose through the centuries until the present outline was formed. It has remained untouched for some three centuries. The main street, the Grand Canal more than 220 feet wide is where the richest Venetian families built their town houses, palaces chiseled and ornamented until the best of them look like jewel boxes, reflecting their images in the waters at their base. There are streets too, behind the façade, forming a maze where the uninitiated would do well to find his way around by compass.

St. Mark's Square, dominated by the great gilded domes and mosaics of incomparable splendor, of the Cathedral of St. Mark, built chiefly in the eleventh century and largely restored in the sixteenth, and by the tall and slender bell tower, the Campanile, is the civic center of Venice. Under the arcades that surround the square are some of the best shops of Venice, displaying the products of Venetian taste and skill

6.   ST. MARK'S CHURCH AND THE LAGOON, VENICE

St. Mark's Cathedral and the palace of the Dukes of Venice look over the lagoon across to St. George's Church, out toward the sea that was once the source of Venice's power and wealth.

— lace, glass, and jewels. Venice, which is the home of 350,000 people, is one of Italy's largest seaports, but tourists have been the greatest source of income since the fortunes of the Venetian Republic began to decline soon after the discovery of the new routes to the Indies during the sixteenth century.

Liguria by the Sea: Columbus's Country

M OST TOURISTS visiting Italy enter the country through one of several gateways. Some come by land, by way of the Alpine passes (some will soon enter by a tunnel under the Alps) from France or from Switzerland, and the first Italian city they see is Milan or Turin. Others prefer the "sunny southern route" by sea, and land at Genoa, Italy's most important port. Genoa, the old rival of Venice in the Middle Ages and the birthplace of Columbus, did at long last succeed in overcoming its great competitor and now handles most of the overseas commerce of northern Italy, as well as a sizable trade for Switzerland and even for south Germany.

The north-west coast of Italy, where Genoa is located, is hemmed in by the deep waters of the Mediterranean and the steep slopes of the Alps and the Apennines. Genoa is almost in the exact middle of the coast of Liguria, as this region is called. The city, with a population of 768,000, is set in a big semi-circular hollow within the coastal mountains, looking out to sea. The port has now recovered from wartime damage, and along the water front you can see the flags of most seafaring countries, and recognize the markings of a dozen European railways.

Genoa is better known to many people, however, as the starting point for journeys east or west along the coast to the eastern or western Riviera of Italy. In beauty and comfort the Italian Riviera equals its more famous continuation to the west, the French Riviera, though it has never had the same publicity. The highway, which offers one of the most delightful and scenic drives imaginable, runs through a string of towns and cities, most of them with a tiny beach of their own, nestled on the mountainside, protected by the mountains from the cold winter winds that sweep across the rest of northern Italy. In this protected little strip of land are Europe's most famous flower gardens. The flower market in such

"Villas" along the Grand Canal, Venice.

One of the many side canals in Venice.

Gondolas on the Grand Canal, Venice.

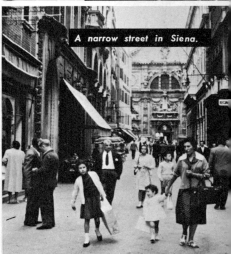
A narrow street in Siena.

Venice's Grand Canal.

San Giorgio Island and Church, Venice

Street scene in Spoleto.

Tenth-Century cathedral in Amalfi.

The cemetery in Pisa.

The Piazza San Marco, Venice.

The straw market in Florence.

The Medici Chapel, Florence.

Ligurian towns as Ventimiglia or San Remo is an unforgettable sight, particularly in early spring when violets, mimosa, and lilacs cover the stalls and the flower vendors' tiny carts.

South-east of Genoa the mountains come so closely down the sea-coast that the railway runs through an almost continuous series of tunnels, and the highway has to swing inland. One might think of that coastal strip as the limit between Genoa, which is still part of northern Italy, and the south of Italy. In a similiar way, behind the Emilian plains there rise the Apennines, a very real barrier to cross for railway and highway, and a separation between the Po Valley and the rest of Italy.

Certainly the tourist bound southward by train, bus, or car from Bologna to Florence and Rome can tell quickly that he has crossed a major divide. The tall poplars of the Po Valley are left behind, and the slender, evergreen cypress takes their place. Instead of intensely cultivated wide plains, much of the landscape is too steep to be used for farming, unless the hillsides and mountain slopes are changed into terraces that appear like giant steps from the distance. The wide range of tones of northern Italy, that runs from the deep emerald green of young rice shoots in the spring to the autumnal golden yellow of ripe corn, disappears. In its place there is a symphony of soft shades: the silvery sheen of olives, the warm russet of ripe grapes, the green of many plants,

The donkey is the beast of burden in the smaller towns and villages, especially in the south. Though small, he is surprisingly strong; he carries flour sacks on his back, wine casks on his sides, and often a rider as well.

particularly the evergreens. Only the summer sky, deep blue, almost black, stands out at all strongly with the white powdery dust of the country roads, and the chalky white of some whitewashed farmhouse.

Donkeys, Not Horses

THE DIFFERENCES between peninsular Italy and northern Italy are important, and while some of them are evident, such as changes in vegetation and farming, and are easily explained in terms of differences of climate and of the nature of the land, others are more subtle and defy simple answers. There is little manufacturing in central and southern Italy, and there are very few regions of industrial production, none comparable to those in the north. Standards of living are different, too. In the north farmhand and industrial worker alike have their own bicycle, if they cannot afford a motorized vehicle of some kind. Further south bicycles become a far more precious possession, and quite a few

people who cannot afford one walk miles each day to work. In the north the beasts of burden are horses or oxen; in central and southern Italy you will still find oxen in the fields and on the roads, but horses are scarce and it is a donkey, small but strong, which carries hay to the barn, grapes to the wine press, and its owner to market.

The regions of the southern part of the Italian peninsula have moved far more slowly toward an economy of manufacturing and advanced scientific farming than northern Italy. Houses and fields, shops in the small towns and market squares almost everywhere have a more old-fashioned look; more things are made by hand, there is less cash in circulation. People are poorer, with fewer possessions than their more fortunate countrymen in the rich farmlands and industrial districts of the north.

One reason for the contrast between northern Italy and the peninsula is history: the north was close to the great European regions of industry and trade, its economy became geared to the rest of Europe during the nineteenth century and even earlier. There was time to pile up surplus capital, used to develop manufacturing, to introduce modern farming practices, such as the use of fertilizers. The peninsula, with the exception of Tuscany, lagged behind. At first it was possible to blame

Politics, the reactionary, backward regimes that ruled most of Italy south of the Apennines. Later, after 1870, when all Italy was united, the north, close to the markets of the continent, with the additional advantages of preferential government treatment in taxes and tariff protection, grew faster and outpaced the central and southern regions. Italy has had a problem in the south — a group of regions poorer than the rest of the country, with fewer resources, feeling ill-treated and ignored ever since it became part of the new, united Italy. Of all problems facing Italy today, none presents more difficulties than that of the lands south of the Apenines. To improve conditions in the south the government has embarked on a huge and ambitious project, for which many billions of lire have been appropriated, to be spent on land reclamation, new roads, mountain dams to provide power and irrigation water.

Tuscany, Painter's Country

THE VISITOR bound for Rome and the south of Italy first meets the world of the Italian peninsula in Tuscany. There is a strangely familiar quality about the Tuscan scene when people see it for the first time: the soft, rolling uplands; vineyards and orchards on the hillside;

At harvest time, oxen rather than tractors are used by farmers in many parts of Italy. Teams of white oxen draw the machines over fields of wheat, others carry cartfuls of sheaves to the threshing floor, and to the barn.

18.   HARVESTING WHEAT, SOUTH ITALY

41

Carrara, in Tuscany, is where the finest Italian marble is quarried. The great sculptors of the past often came here to pick out a particularly fine block of marble, the raw material of great statues and monuments.

20. MARBLE QUARRY AT CARRARA, TUSCANY

wheatfields in the valley; cypresses standing guard in front of handsome old houses set on lonely hilltops; and over it all a clear, strong light. This is a scene found in hundreds of Renaissance paintings: the view from a tiny window behind the subject's head in a portrait, the background for a group of people, holy personages or worldly shepherds, out in the open on a lovely day. Tuscany, more than any other part of Italy, is identified with the Renaissance, and its cities and towns, its hillsides and winding, pleasant valleys, the wide views from the hilltop villages, are part of the artistic heritage that the Renaissance has given to the world.

The idyllic picture of a Tuscan shepherd playing his flute on a hillside does not quite cover the realities of today, however. Tuscany is one of Italy's best farming regions, especially famous for the Chianti wine district, the country's leading commercial wine producer. It is also the region where tenant farming has persisted for centuries, and where much of the land is still owned by absentee landlords. The conflict between owner and tenant, always near the surface, became a major problem on the local and national scene immediately after World War II. The debate over tenancy contracts has been a leading issue in Italian politics ever since 1945, and a solution that would please landlord and tenant at the same time is as far away as ever.

FLORENCE

STADIUM

Campo di Marte

to Greve

Via G. Orsini

V. Gioberti

PIAZZA
DONATELLO

PIAZZA
BECCARIA

Vle. Amendola

Arno

L. Zecca

Via Tripoli

PIAZZALE MICHELANGELO

V. Gramsci

CATHEDRAL OF
SANTA MARIA
DEL FIORE

Piazza del Duomo

UNIVERSITY

V. Alfani

MEDICI-
RICCARDI
PALACE

V. Cerretani

BAPISTERY OF
SAN GIOVANNI

V. Corso

PALAZZO
VECCHIO

PALAZZO
UFFIZI
(Gallery)

Piazza della
Signoria

L. Diaz

PONTE
VECCHIO

Lungarno Serristori

to Bologna

Viale Lavagnini

Viale Filippo Strozzi

Via F. Strozzi

FORTEZZA
DA BASSO

CENTRAL
STATION

Prato

Lungarno Amer. Vespucci

River

to Empoli

V. Pisana

PALAZZO
PITTI

Via Serragli

Boboli
Gardens

to Siena

If It Is Made of Leather, You Can Buy It in Florence

FLORENCE, (437,000 inhabitants), of all Tuscan cities, is the most famous and as a home of arts and crafts it has been a leader among Italian cities for centuries. Built along the banks of the winding Arno River, ever since the Middle Ages Florence has been known as a city of Bridges. World War II, while leaving the rest of the city untouched destroyed the bridges in its wake. Only the oldest called the "Ponte Vecchio", the Old Bridge built in medieval times, remained standing. With rows of shops on either side where Florentine silver, leather, and jewels tempt the passer-by, the Old Bridge is a bit of the Middle Ages, a tiny world of its own.

During the flowering of the Renaissance, Florence was the richest Italian city and the wealth of its great families supported the leading artists of the time. The heart of Florence is filled with palaces, churches, and art galleries. The main square, set below the high tower of the fourteenth-century City Hall, with an open-air gallery of statues, and

11.   PONTE VECCHIO, FLORENCE

Florence is a river town, and the picturesque Ponte Vecchio, Old Bridge, spanning the Arno River, is one of its main attractions. It is lined with tiny shops on both sides, and thronged with pedestrians.

This is the great dining hall in the Pitti Palace, Florence.

Siena in central Italy is noted for its wine and marble. The home where St. Catherine of Siena was born is located here and is a much-frequented shrine.

the Uffizi Museum which houses the best-known collection of Renaissance paintings, is an unending source of delight for Florentine and visitor alike. Sitting on the terraces of cafés, they watch the passing parade morning and evening, in a setting where every line of every building is as clear-cut and precise as if worked in precious stone by a master-craftsman's hand.

Tuscany during the Middle Ages saw the rise of as many tiny republics as there were hilltop towns and ambitious, clever men in those towns. And though every one of those small city-states later fell before

The Leaning Tower, a twelfth-century Campanile, 180 feet high and fourteen feet out of the perpendicular, is Pisa's trade-mark, and the best-known landmark of Italy. Next to it stands the gleaming marble mass of the Cathedral, with its great bronze doors.

the power of the Florentine Medici family, the towns retained much of their beauty. In some, the monuments built to please both God and their builder stand in their beauty still, as in Pisa with its great Campanile called the Leaning Tower, its 900-year-old Cathedral and eleventh-century Baptistery, and Siena, near Florence, with one of the earliest great Tuscan Gothic churches. Others kept shrinking within their walls; their people just could not afford to build new houses and new churches. As a result, some of these towns are like museums of the past, with hardly a new building added since the fifteenth century.

Assisi, the Town of St. Francis

S OUTH OF TUSCANY, road and railway pass from the valley of the Arno to that of the Tiber, to the regions of Umbria and of Lazio. Umbria lies close to the middle of the Italian peninsula. It is a tiny region, one that has become famous through the actions and words of its most famous native son, St. Francis of Assisi.

St. Francis was born in the town of Assisi in 1182. The ancient little city is a nest of houses perched on a hillside, overlooking the wide valley of the Tiber. St. Francis was the most gentle of all the great figures of the Church; his vows of poverty, his preaching of Christian compassion toward one's fellow human beings as well as toward the dumb creatures, have never been forgotten. The town of his birth, where he now lies buried in a large and proud cathedral built in the thirteenth century, still has about it an air of friendliness that would be hard to match anywhere in Italy or in Europe. Many thousands of pilgrims come to commemorate him every year.

South-east from Umbria stretch the craggy ranges of the Apennines, southern Italy — the Marche, Abruzzi, Molise, Basilicata. These are regions vastly different from the popular conception of Italy as the sunny land of happy, singing farmers, and of cities rich in their artistic heritage. The interior of the Italian peninsula is harsh country where high mountains, steep valleys, barren soils, and a climate of snowy, cold winters and scorchingly hot, bone-dry summers discourage farming, rule out leisure, and have little to offer to visitors in search of art and beauty.

Two of the most successful books by contemporary Italian writers, Silone's *Fontamara* and Levi's *Christ Stopped at Eboli*, deal with this Italy that stretches from the gates of Rome and Assisi to the southern end of the peninsula. For the most part these lands were ruled by Spain for three centuries prior to the rise of united Italy. They were neglected by the state, devoid of decent roads, infested by bandits, off the beaten track.

Festivals and Folk Dress in the South

OVER MUCH of southern Italy tiny farms are carved out of mountain slopes. Men raise corn, vegetables, and wheat on handkerchief-sized terraces. Every spring great flocks of sheep are driven up to the high mountain meadows where there is enough rain to grow a good cover of grass. Summer over, the flocks are moved once more, down toward the coastal plains, to winter pasture.

The peasants who look after sheep and goats still lead the life of nomads, moving from lowland winter pasture to upland summer grazing with their flocks. Here they are shown during the winter, in front of their thatched hut, their dogs lounging in the sun.

Carnival is festival time in Italy. Disguised by mask or paint, townsfolk throng the streets of Frascati, a hill town near Rome, while large papier-mâché figures of King Carnival and his court are carried around.

The south is Old Italy. Every once in a while one catches a glimpse of a brilliant, hand-embroidered skirt, or of a lacy cap beneath the black shawls women wear in the wintertime. The heavy fur-lined capes men wrap themselves in have big, handsome silver buttons. Factory-made clothing has not completely driven out the homespun, and on holidays especially you can see something of the bright, traditional folk dress.

Festivals are popular everywhere in Italy. But in the south they take on even greater importance when the people get away from the hard chores of flock and farm, and enjoy the gaiety and music of a holiday. These "feste" go back to the earliest days of Christianity, and celebrate the local patron saint or some high holiday, Christmas or Easter. Many festivals go even beyond the origins of Christianity, and represent pagan celebrations of spring planting and harvesting, now devoted to the familiar figures of the Christian calendar.

On certain days, the citizens of Italian towns dress up in historic costumes, to celebrate events in their local history. These processions look like great Renaissance paintings come to life, and the citizens wear their motley garb proudly, much as if it was their everyday attire.

24.   PROCESSION IN COSTUMES, FLORENCE

For centuries most of the land in southern Italy was owned by noble families in large estates. There was not enough land to feed a growing population. The late nineteenth century and the first years of the twentieth were the times when Italians left their homeland by the million and sought their fortune overseas, frequently in the Americas or in Australia. A tourist journeying in southern Italy will find someone who speaks English in nearly every village, someone who saved his earnings through years of hard work, and returned to his village, a man of means by local standards.

Landed Estates Replaced by Peasant Farmers

I MMEDIATELY after World War II, when Italy got rid of Fascism and political arguments once more were carried on in the open, the poverty of the southern peasant became a matter of national concern. Since 1950 the Italian government has been spending astronomical sums each year in southern Italy to improve the lot of its people. Called the Cassa program, from Cassa per Il Mezzogiorno (Fund for the Development of the South), it has involved the appropriation of more than a thousand billion lire on more than 200,000 separate projects involving roads, dams, schools, hotels, and many more. This has probably been the most spectacular undertaking in Italy in many decades. The large landed estates are now broken up. Most of their holdings were sold to new owners who did not own land before and who now have farms with the help of a government loan. New roads were built to reach villages that were accessible only on donkeys or on foot; new villages were developed to bring the farmer close to his land, and cut the time taken in walking miles to the fields morning and night; new medical services are available; new schools for the children and for adult education. For the first time in centuries the people of southern Italy are reaping some benefit.

Most of Italy south of Rome would fit the description given here, with only two exceptions: the Naples region on the west coast, and Apulia on the east coast. Not that either of these two is particularly prosperous — on the contrary; because they are more densely settled, their problems, too, are serious. But the Naples region and Apulia do have certain resources which the rest of the south does not possess. And these two regions have one more feature in common, one they share with Sicily;

This herd of goats, the poor man's cows, stopped in the Sicilian town of Gela, on its way to pasture. They are taking a "break" by the roadside, while the more adventurous goats are exploring behind the fence.

Any sunny day is washday in Italy. Here, women take their wash to the community "launderette" in Terni. There is plenty of clear running water, a warm sun to dry the clothes, and good company, too.

they are lands with the atmosphere of ancient Greece, lands where most of the cities and towns were founded by Greeks over 2,000 years ago, and many still bear their ancient Greek name.

Oranges, Volcanoes and Fish: Naples

THE NAPLES region is Italy's most densely populated, with Naples itself claiming a population of nearly 1.2 million, surrounded by dozens of smaller cities and towns. It is also one of the more striking regions of Italy. It is a narrow sickle-shaped area, surrounding the Bay of Naples and dominated by the tall cone of Mt. Vesuvius, the only active volcano on the mainland of Europe. Naples is now Italy's third-largest city and its second port. It is a city lively even by Italian stand-

Village streets are narrow, cobblestoned passageways between tall stone houses. People like to sit in the sun, enjoying an hour of warmth during a winter day.

ards; its streets, most of them narrow, wind their way between the hills and the sea, washing hangs high above the heads of the pedestrians in all but the most expensive parts, and there is a constant stream of cars, carts, trucks, tramcars, buses, and donkeys, clanking and honking and braying through most of the day. The shops display such characteristic products of Naples as cameos, enamel brooches and pins and rings, necklaces and bracelets of coral. At Christmas time all the streets of the older parts of the city become a vast outdoor display of tiny figures, sold by the thousand, of the Italian crèche, where the Christ Child, surrounded by the Holy Family, shepherds, kings from the Orient, and farmers from the countryside, sleeps in a tiny hut of wood or papier-mâché.

Outside Naples the fertile volcanic ash of Vesuvius that once buried Pompeii under a thick, searing and suffocating blanket of volcanic ash now supports farms that grow vegetables and hemp, wheat and fruit, oranges and lemons. The bay teems with all kinds of fish and the restaurants on the Naples water front serve the best seafood in Italy. On the south end of the Bay of Naples the steep, rocky cape of Sorrento stands out to sea; beyond it and out of sight lies the most spectacular of all Italian coasts, the Amalfi coast. The drive along the shore called the Amalfi Drive is probably the most breathtakingly scenic stretch of highway in Europe. Amalfi, the old seafaring republic of the Middle Ages, is a tiny town of fishermen today, clinging to the steep mountain wall that towers above it, looking down on a beach barely large enough for the smallest of fishing barges.

Offshore, and cutting off the Bay of Naples from the open Mediterranean, are two islands, Capri and Ischia. Ischia is an ancient, extinct volcano and on its slopes people raise some of the best oranges and grapes of Italy. Capri is an almost barren rock, where drinking water has to be brought by tanker from the mainland and carefully kept in cisterns. During the last twenty years it has become one of Europe's

17.　　　　　　　　　RUINS OF POMPEII

When Vesuvius buried the city of Pompeii under its ashes, in 79 A.D., an entire Roman town was saved for posterity, whose houses, streets, temples, and markets, now excavated, are a fine image of what life was like in Roman times.

21.   CAPRI SHORELINE

The rocky shores of "the Isle of Capri", near Naples, fall steeply to
the Mediterranean. Above, on the slopes, are villas of famous
actors and exiled kings, as well as the houses of the farmers and
fishermen of Capri.

Positano is a delightful bathing resort on the Gulf of Salerno.

The heart of all Italian towns is the central square, the *piazza*, with its church, shops, and open-air cafés. This is the piazza of Capri, the popular island resort near Naples, full of tourists watching the passing parade.

most popular resorts, where ex-kings and film stars, writers, and designers of fashionable clothing can be seen chatting in the cafés on the tiny "piazza".

Apulia: Limestone, Olives, and Fruit

APULIA, the south-eastern part of the peninsula, the heel of the boot, overlooking the Adriatic Sea from the west, and the Gulf of Taranto from the north, is quite different from the Naples region. Most of it is a gently rolling plateau, underlain by limestone, covered by farmland and pasture. Along the seacoast there is a belt of orchards famous for almonds, peaches, apples, and plums; inland are wheatfields, groves of olives, and wide-open pasture.

Apulia was much loved by Frederick II, a fabulous figure of the Middle Ages — a German Emperor who loved only Italy, who, when Christian and Moslem were at each other's throats, was equally at home in the Christian and in the Moslem world. Frederick II was one of the greatest builders Italy has known and from the mellow, reddish-yellow limestone of Apulia his masons and architects built castles and cathedrals that make a visit to the region most worthwhile.

William the Conqueror's Cousins Did Well in Sicily

SICILY, THE BIG TRIANGULAR island just off the toe of Italy, with an area of about 10,000 square miles, has a population of 4.9 million, making it the most densely populated island in the Mediterranean. It has known every form of rule in its long history. Greek city-states were founded there 700 years before Christ. Roman governors controlled it for centuries, eager to ship the rich wheat harvest of the island to the

These beehive-shaped structures are stables, of the form called *trullo*, a form that is thousands of years old and still used in Apulia. Stables, whitewashed farmhouse, outdoor oven, are all made of local limestone, cut by hand.

Wine jugs, jars for olive oil, and even water pitchers are made by the village potter, in shapes that have not changed since Greek and Roman days. Here, in an Apulian village, you can see rows of pottery being set out to dry under the hot southern sun.

hungry crowds of Rome. Later, Arab soldiers conquered the island; Arab farmers brought with them the art of irrigation; Arab artisans built mosques and palaces for their kings. In the eleventh century Norman knights made Sicily's Golden Age; their mosaic-covered cathedrals, and palaces ornamented with rare Oriental ceilings and unusual marbles are still breath-taking. Nine hundred years ago Palermo, Sicily's capital, a city now of 600,000 people, was the richest, most prosperous city of the Mediterranean, where Christian, Moslem, and Jew worked side by side under the protection of Norman conquerors, the same people whose

A cart can be a handsome thing as well as a useful one. In Sicily, two artisans are decorating a farmer's cart in all the hues of the rainbow, with figures that vary from the Knights of the Round Table to film actresses of today.

High on a windswept hill, overlooking the coast of Sicily, stands this row of Greek columns. Once it was a temple where the merchants of the nearby Greek city, now called Agrigento, went to worship.

It's harvest time in the orange groves that cover the slopes of Mount Etna, the great Sicilian volcano. The golden oranges look like Christmas tree ornaments, set against a deep blue sky.

10.　　　ORANGE GROVES, SICILY

cousins and brothers had conquered England at about the same time. One has to look behind the façades of Palermo and other Sicilian towns to find memories of that great age, but the quest is likely to be rewarding.

Sicily has dramatic variety of terrain and character. The interior of the island is chiefly a rugged, lonely land of isolated villages, rolling wheat fields, and craggy mountains that rise to a dramatic climax in the towering peak of Mount Etna, more than 10,000 feet high, a recently active volcano. But along the shore the land is densely settled, and seaside towns alternate with orange groves and farms. Under the special statute that gave Sicily a large measure of self-government in 1946, the island's hitherto neglected resources are slowly being developed. It has long been one of the world's great producers of sulphur, accounting for 1.5 million metric tons a year, two-thirds of all produced in Italy. But in recent years Sicily has surged ahead in other ways: its oil production is now about 2 million tons a year, natural gas production has increased many-fold, and new hydro-electric installations in the mountains are providing much-needed new sources of power, as well as water for the extension of irrigation.

Shepherds, Cork Trees, and Coal Mines

M OST OF SARDINIA, Italy's second largest island, is mountainous, except for a narrow plain, the Campidano, in the south-west corner of the island. The climate is very dry and irrigation is indispensable to any successful farming.

Sardinia's rugged 9,200 square miles support about 1.4 million people engaged primarily in wresting a modest living from sheep and cork oaks. But in the last few years Sardinia has entered the early stages of a developing economic and cultural boom with several facets. Italy's expanding industry has found urgent need for the island's minerals: coal,

The strange, striking stripes on the façade of this tiny church in Sardinia represent a style once popular in Tuscany. This church used to serve a thriving community in the past; now the area is empty of people, and the church comes to life only one Sunday during the year.

25.   MEDIEVAL CHURCH IN SARDINIA

zinc, lead, copper, and others less well known. Important land reclamation projects have drained unhealthy marshes and provided water for irrigation, adding about 200,000 acres to the island's cultivated fields.

But more than anything else, convenient air travel from the Italian mainland has helped "discover" Sardinia for an increasing stream of tourists. It has become one of those distinctive, picturesque corners of the world that knowing visitors recommend as still uncrowded and unspoiled.

For the mounting stream of tourists new hotels and inns have been opened, roads improved, and itineraries arranged.

After World War II the United Nations made it possible, through its support of a special government agency, to carry out in Sardinia one of the most spectacular anti-malaria campaigns ever seen. Special teams sprayed every house, every ruin, every creek, every sheep pen on the island with DDT, and in three years' time malaria disappeared. With this menace removed, the people of the island are working under better conditions, agriculture is improving, and visitors are welcome. The lonely, rugged mountains; the unusual prehistoric towers that ring all coasts of the island, the *nuraghi;* the splendid folk costumes so proudly worn on festival days by men and women, and the warm hospitality Sardianians offer to strangers, should make Sardinia the goal of people in quest of interesting places off the beaten path. Soon people using the island's lonely roads may be surprised to see a remarkable sight, a missile launching pad, developed with the co-operation of Italian and foreign interests, at a cost of many millions of dollars.

Italy and the Free World

IN MANY WAYS Italy is a poor land; it lacks several of the metals, minerals, and fuels that are vital in our industrial age. It is afflicted with poor soils and too little rain. But it has one great asset — the people. Italians work hard, they work long hours, they have artistic talent, inventiveness, skills inherited from generations of great artists and superb craftsmen. And they love their country. The combination of skills, energy, and imagination associated in a surging national drive is reaping its reward. In its industrial production Italy is reaching new levels each year. Steel production has climbed to 9 million metric tons. Its merchant marine, one of the world's great fleets, has 3,800 vessels, accounting for more than 5 million gross tons. Land reform and better farming methods are adding hundreds of thousands of acres to fields, the products of many of which are increasingly finding world markets.

But of particular economic importance is the growing army of visitors who swarm to Italy from every corner of the world, about 18 million foreign visitors a year. The money they bring in represents an appreciable part of the national revenue.

Italy's partnership in defending western Europe is an established fact now. After a brief period when Italy was isolated from the free world, it is once more very much part of that world. In 1955 Italy joined the United Nations, and subsequently became an active partner in NATO. It took signficant leadership in the establishment of both the European Economic Community (Common Market) and the European Atomic Energy Community, both established by treaty signed at Rome in 1957.

Some Important Dates in Italian History

B.C.	760–	Greek colonies in south Italy and Sicily
	753	Rome founded, according to tradition
	102–44	Julius Caesar
B.C.	31–	
A.D.	14	Augustus, first Roman Emperor
	100–180	Golden Age of Roman Empire
	306–337	Constantine the Great — Christianity religion of Roman Empire

410	Barbarians sack Rome
476	Last Roman Emperor loses his throne
586	Venice becomes a city
800	Charlemagne, a Frank, becomes Emperor, crowned in Rome by the Pope
1211–1250	Frederick II, Emperor, patron of arts
1265–1321	Dante Alighieri, author of "Divine Comedy," first great Italian poet
1434–1494	Golden Age of Florence under the Medici
1452–1519	Leonardo da Vinci
1475–1564	Michelangelo Buonarroti
1494–1559	Continuous foreign invasions of Italy, ending in foreign conquest
1564–1642	Galileo Galilei
1805–1872	Giuseppe Mazzini
1807–1882	Giuseppe Garibaldi
1810–1861	Camillo Count Cavour
1848–1870	Italian Wars of Independence
1870	Rome becomes capital of united Italy
1849–1878	Victor Emmanuel II, King of Italy
1915	Italy entered World War I, on side of Allies
1922	Benito Mussolini became Prime Minister
1929	Lateran Treaty, reconciliation of Italy and the Pope
1935–1936	Ethiopian War
1940	Italy entered World War II on German side
1943	Italy surrendered, fought on with Allies; Fascists continued fighting on German side until 1945
1946	Plebiscite ends kingdom, proclaims Italian Republic
1955	Italy joins the United Nations
1957	Treaty establishing both the European Economic Community (Common Market) of six European nations, and the European Atomic Energy Community signed in Rome, with Italy a full member
1960	Italy plays host to the Olympic Games at Rome
1961	Centenary celebrations of Italian unity, at Turin

Handy Words and Phrases in Italian

English	Italian
Hello!	Buon giorno!
Hello (on a telephone).	Pronto.
Good evening, night.	Buona sera, notte.
How much is this?	Quanto costa?
Please.	Prego.
Thank you (very much).	Grazie (Tante grazie).
Do you speak English?	Parla inglese?
Where is (the station).	Dov'è (la stazione).
Straight ahead.	Sempre dritto.
To the right.	Sulla destra.
To the left.	Sulla sinistra.
Where is the toilet?	Dov'è il gabinetto?
The bill, please.	Il conto, per favore.
Coffee (with milk).	Caffè (con latte).
Tea, milk, chocolate.	Tè, latte, cioccolato.
Veal, chicken, fish.	Vitello, pollo, pesce.
Soup, dessert.	Zuppa, dolce.
Bread, wine, beer, water.	Pane, vino, birra, acqua.
Any kind of spaghetti.	Pasta.
Breakfast, lunch, dinner.	Colazione, pranzo, cena.
Film show.	Cinematografo.
Post, telegraph office.	Ufficio poste, telegrafi.
Hotel room (with bath).	Camera (con bagno).
With running water.	Con acqua corrente.
Hot, cold.	Caldo, freddo.
Bus (local).	Autobus.
Bus (long distance).	Autopullman, corriera.
Tramcar, bus stop.	Fermata per tranvia, per autobus.
How are you?	Come sta?
Fine, thank you.	Bene, grazie.
Good-by.	Arrivederci.